Picturing Fayette

A Nineteenth-Century Company Town

by

Fred and Donna Winters

Picturing Fayette, A Nineteenth-Century Company Town
Copyright © 2013 by Fred and Donna Winters

Bigwater Publishing LLC
P.O. Box 85, Garden, MI 49835

ISBN 0-923048-54-5
ISBN 978-0-923048-54-9

Town Hall
Iron Port, Escanaba
October 4, 1879
The Town Hall is to be converted into a store room; a misfortune to the town, as it is the only place here suitable for large assemblages.

THE HOTEL

Iron Port, Escanaba, June 2, 1877

Last Wednesday evening, a farewell supper was given at the Fayette House, to Mr. H. Van Allen, a gentleman who has been in the employ of the Jackson Iron Co. for some time. It is reported as a very pleasant affair. An address was made by Rev. T. J. MacMurray, and responded to by Mr. Allen. The occasion was enlivened by singing, varied by speeches from Messrs. J. B. Kitchen, W. M. Dogget, A.S. Kitchen, J. Meham, and Dr. Bellows. Our space forbids us to give the speeches in detail, as we would wish.

Iron Port, Escanaba, May 17, 1879

Our old friend Sawbridge is still running the Fayette House and trying to serve the public to the best of his knowledge and belief. He complains however of a dryness in the times, probably owing to the ukase [sic] promulgated by the powers that be, against the issuing of that thirst quenching beverage called beer. But he still gets up as good a meal as ever and his beds are a perfect haven of rest for the weary.

Iron Herald, Negaunee
Saturday, December 13, 1879
Jerry Crosby had a narrow escape from death, at the furnace, one day last week. He was buried under three feet of ore at the bottom of the hopper used for weighing the crushed ore. It required an hour to dig him out, but he was none the worse for the tumble, except some slight bruises.

Iron Port, Escanaba
October 4, 1879
The Fayette furnace turned out 220½ tons of iron during the week ending Sept. 27.

THE MACHINE SHOP was one of the first buildings constructed and was of dolomite which made it fireproof. It contained a metal lathe, iron planer, and standing drill used by machinists to keep the furnace and railroad in operation. A small steam engine in the shop ran off steam from the furnace and operated the equipment. Sometimes, accidents befell the machine shop workers:

Iron Port, Escanaba, September 21, 1878. Geo. Schiling, of Fayette, unfortunately got his hand caught in the iron planer which produced a cominated fracture of the metacarpus. He is under the care of Dr. C. J. Bellows, who will use his best endeavors to save the injured member.

Above: Company Store and Warehouse

Company Office

Once a month clerks issued wages to Jackson Iron Company employees who stood in line to collect their pay. Deductions for rent, store purchases, and medical fees were first deducted from earnings, leaving some laborers with but a few cents for an entire month's hard work.

Superintendent's House

Escanaba Tribune
June 17, 1876
Nearly three years since Mr. Kitchen [Superintendent] succeeded Mr. Charles Rhodes—for some years in charge—and under its present able management, everything moves like clockwork. (May it never need winding up.)

Escanaba Iron Port
Saturday, April 27, 1889
The Calumet of Tuesday made an attack on Mr. Saunders, superintendent of the Jackson Iron Co's Business at Fayette, accusing him of bulldozing or attempting to bulldoze the company's employees at the late township election and of having discharged a number of them because of the course they took at that time.

Managers' Homes

THE DOCTOR'S HOUSE

Schoolcraft County Pioneer, Manistique, February 6, 1884
Last week a man named Carr, while engaged in a friendly wrestling match with a companion, nearby a team of horses, at kiln no. 5, near Fayette, frightened one of the horses, who viciously kicked the young man in the head, fracturing his skull. Doctors Budd and Davis were called and at last accounts it was thought that the young man might recover.

Iron Port, Escanaba, October 11, 1879

Dr. Budd's raffle came off as per programme Friday night. The dance (no raffle without a dance) was well attended, and is said, by those who were there, to have been gorgeous in the extreme. The raffle was for a pole cutter, and Dr. Bellows the winner. He believes in raffles, and now possesses the finest winter rig in the U. P. It is said to have cost $175.

"The huts were built on the very edge of the street. In front and around them, hens scratched, and hogs wallowed in the mire… Oh, the stench…and the filthy, ragged children!"
Snail-Shell Harbor, J.H. Langille

Iron Port, Escanaba October 4, 1879 Fayette is not a model of cleanliness, and it's difficult to keep everything in apple pie order but there is no excuse for that back alley. [A reference to the alley behind the log cabins.]

Escanaba Tribune, September 24, 1870
Fears were entertained that the supply of charcoal would fall short, but with extraordinary exertions, they now have another set of kilns ready, and supply will be kept up.

Mining Journal, Marquette, December 30, 1876
The Fayette Furnace was badly damaged by fire on Friday night of last week. As nearly as we can ascertain, one of the arches gave out, & the iron breaking out over the dam, set the whole concern on fire.

Schoolcraft County Pioneer, Manistique
June 27, 1883
Last Monday G.H. Harris met with quite an accident: one of his teams at the kilns got stuck with a load of wood, and he tried to help them out, got hold of one of the four wheels by the spokes, to start up the wagon, the team started to one side, and caught his hand between the wheel and the iron stake holder, jamming it badly. Doctor Davis dressed the wound. He will be out again in 3 or 4 days as smart as ever.

Iron Port, Escanaba, June 14, 1879
"Drowned! Six Lives Lost Beneath the Waves!"
On Monday afternoon about four o'clock a heavy squall came from the west-north-west.
About that time a sailboat was seen from Fayette approaching the shore. The helmsman
appeared to be steering wildly, and its course when the squall struck was very erratic.
There seemed to be several men and also a woman in the boat. When within about a mile
from shore screams and cries were heard from the occupants. Almost immediately
afterwards the boat swamped with its load and disappeared. The Jackson Iron Company's
tug Joe Harris, Capt. Colwell, went immediately to the scene of disaster…

20

The *Denis Sullivan* from Milwaukee

Iron Port, **Escanaba, Nov. 19, 1887**
A Sailor belonging to the crew of the *Kitchen* fell through the hatch into the hold and was severely injured.

Schoolcraft County Pioneer, Manistique, [Date unknown.]
Billie Pinchin met with quite an accident last Friday while hauling coal from the kilns to the [Fayette] furnace. It appears that the shaft of his truck broke, and that frightened the horse, who jumped and upset the coal buggy, lodged Billie in the mud, and headed for the barn. Nobody got hurt, but Billie had the fun of scraping the mud off his clothes. In about 15 minutes the horse was hitched up to another truck, and Billie was on duty again as if nothing had ever happened.

Iron Port, Escanaba
September 27, 1879
There are more carriages and
wheeled vehicles in Fayette than in
any other town of its size on the
peninsula.

www.ingramcontent.com/pod-product-compliance
Lightning Source LLC
Chambersburg PA
CBHW042112040426
42448CB00002B/239